D is for Darcy
Not Dyslexia

Abigail Griebelbauer

Illustrations by Cecilia Edwards

Published by The Passage Press
For orders, please email info@thepassagepress.com

Cover design and illustrations by
Cecilia Edwards

D is for Darcy Not Dyslexia / Abigail Griebelbauer
The art fair is in two weeks! Darcy still isn't done with her masterpiece and reading class is next. What is she going to do? Reading is her hardest class! Follow along as her teacher, Miss Williams, and her friend, Clara, encourage her to keep trying. Does Darcy listen to their advice or does her dyslexia stop her from doing things she loves?

Hardback ISBN-13: 978-1-7357777-0-2
Paperback ISBN-13: 978-1-7357777-1-9
eBook ISBN-13: 978-1-7357777-2-6

Library of Congress Control Number: 2020919464

Second Edition.
First Edition: October 2020

Dedication

Author Dedication

To my mother and father who recognize the strengths and struggles of dyslexia.

To my brother for supporting me through creating this book and running a business.

To my friends who have always been by my side to lend a helping hand, cry during the difficult times, and celebrate all the wins.

Illustrator Dedication

To Phillip, my brother, who once told me that I was like a modern-day Wonder Woman.

To my mom, for supporting the creativity even when it took over the dining room table...sofa... kitchen counter...bedroom...and living room.

To my dad, who was the first one to see me as an artist.

"Okay, class!" Miss Williams said. "Remember to turn in your homework on your way to art class with Mr. Clark."

Darcy set her homework on Miss Williams' desk and then got in line with her friend, Clara.

"What is your project for the art fair this year?" Clara asked.

"It's a surprise," Darcy said. "I'm not ready to show it to anyone. Who do you think will go to the state competition this year?"

Clara smiled. "I think you will," she said.

Darcy was having **so much fun** working on her art project that she barely felt the time passing. Before she knew it, she heard Mr. Clark say, "There are five minutes left, so let's clean up."

Clara turned to Darcy. "Did you finish the reading homework last night?" she asked.

Darcy nodded. She had done the homework, but it hadn't been easy.

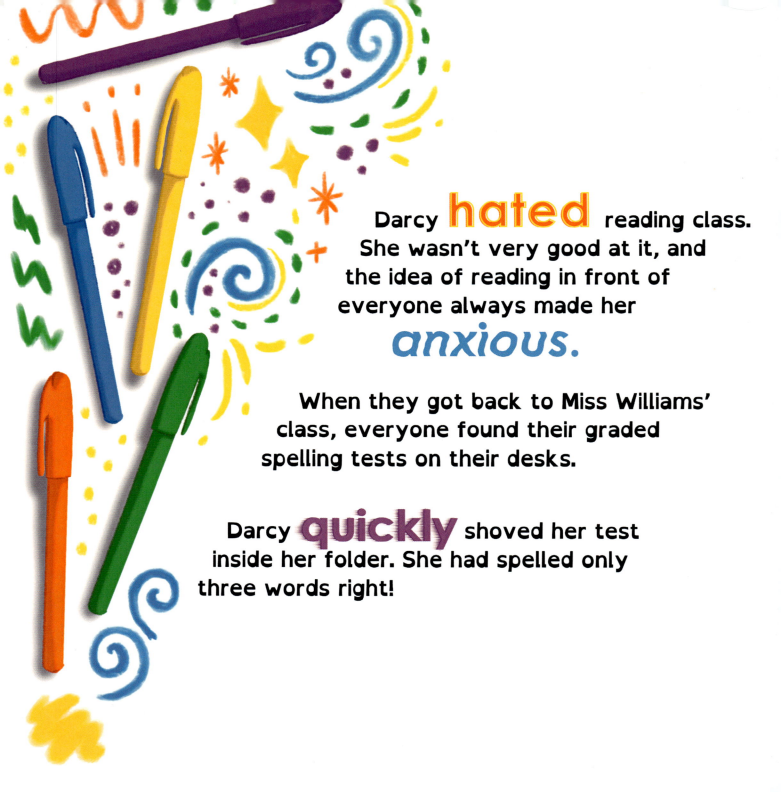

Darcy **hated** reading class. She wasn't very good at it, and the idea of reading in front of everyone always made her *anxious.*

When they got back to Miss Williams' class, everyone found their graded spelling tests on their desks.

Darcy **quickly** shoved her test inside her folder. She had spelled only three words right!

"All right," Miss Williams said. "Get out your reading books and turn to page 188." Darcy opened her reading book. She tried to follow along, but **she kept getting lost.**

She looked for words that she knew to help find her place, but by the time she found them, the rest of the class had moved on.

She didn't understand anything that was being read. *Why is everyone reading so quickly?* she wondered. *Why isn't this hard for them? Where are we?*

"It's your turn, Darcy," Miss Williams said.

Darcy's heart began **beating so loudly** she thought her classmates across the room could hear it.

"Do you know where we are?" Miss Williams asked.

Darcy nodded and slowly began to read,

"The s-u-n sh-i-n-ed br-i-gh-t be-h-in-d the tr-ees. It w-as a b-ea-u-ti-f-ul s-i-gh-t to s-ee."

After two sentences, Miss Williams said, "Great job, Darcy. Annie, you're up."

Darcy slumped back in her chair, **embarrassed.**

She hated reading aloud. It was the worst part of every school day, and she always ended up disappointed in herself because she did not read like everyone else.

Why am I the only one who struggles? Darcy thought.

The bell rang and the rest of the class
rushed outside for recess. Darcy
was halfway out the door when
Miss Williams stopped her.

"Darcy, you've been working
hard on your reading, and
I can see you improving.

Keep up your
hard work," she said.

Darcy sighed and said,
"Why is reading so hard for me?"

"Everyone has different
strengths, and you will find
yours," said Miss Williams.

"Some brains think
differently.

This can make learning to read take longer.
We just need to find ways that help you.
You have lots of strengths – like art.
I, for one, am looking forward to
seeing your piece at the art fair."

"Thank you," Darcy said and she
headed out to recess.

"There you are!" Clara said when Darcy came outside. "You did such a great job reading today!

I can tell you're working hard."

"Thanks, Clara," Darcy said. Then to herself, she thought *Maybe Miss Williams and Clara are right. Maybe I am getting better!*

Over the next two weeks, Darcy tried to focus on her reading. But she focused even more on her art project.

Finally, the day of the art fair arrived. Darcy was so nervous. Only four pieces would earn a ribbon. She ran into the room to see how she had done.

Darcy found her project.

There was no ribbon in sight. **Tears** fell down her face. She knew she'd done her best, but it hadn't been enough.

"Wow, your piece is amazing!" Clara said, coming up behind her. "I think it is the best project out of all of them."

"Thanks," Darcy said. "But I still lost."

Just then, a voice boomed from the stage. It was the principal. "I'd like to thank everyone for coming," she said. "And now, the moment you've all been waiting for: the **big winner** who will go on to the state competition is...

... Darcy Wright!"

Darcy couldn't believe it! She had won after all! Looking around, Darcy could see Miss Williams and Clara clapping and cheering for her.

Miss Williams was right. Art was one of her strengths. And if she worked at it, maybe reading could be one, too. One thing was for sure,

she wasn't giving up!

About the Author

Abigail Griebelbauer goes by many names. Most people in her life just call her Abby, while her campers from summer camp called her "Tinkerbell" or "Tink." Her students simply called her "Miss G." She loves spending time with loved ones, traveling the world, learning new things, and playing board games. Abigail is dyslexic, which inspired her to write this children's book, based in part on her own school experiences. In college, she realized that being dyslexic was one of her strengths. Being dyslexic helped her develop the gifts of patience, empathy, creativity, and the understanding that everyone's brain works differently.

About the Illustrator

Some of Cecilia's earliest memories are of drawing and painting at an easel in the kitchen while her parents cooked dinner, and since then, she hasn't been able to stop creating! Her lifelong love for art has led to some pretty cool opportunities, like working at a museum in London, designing wedding invitations for her friends, and having her artwork featured on BBC. After living in London for a while, she now lives in the beautiful mountains of Tennessee and likes to spend her free time watching 1980s movies with her brother, Phillip, and getting snuggles from their four cats!

Author's Note

Dear Readers,

    I created this book because when I was growing up, I didn't see any characters in books who struggled in class like me. I didn't see any characters who felt the way I did when reading. I hope that Darcy becomes this character for children all over the world. In this story, I wanted to include the concept that people with dyslexia can become great readers with more time and practice. Personally, I improved my reading most while studying abroad in college. This is also where I met one of my best friends, Cecilia, the illustrator of this book.

    Now we are both working hard to create books like this one to start conversations about disabilities in homes and schools. We are creating a series to make sure all children see themselves in characters in books and are able to share their feelings. Representation matters in all aspects whether it be race, ethnicity, or disability. To help spread this message, please share this book with people in your life. Word of mouth will be the best way to get this message to the world.

    Lastly, the following pages are activity pages. If any printed or additional copies are needed, please visit The Passage Press website. On the last page, you will find a list of discussion questions. We encourage you to learn more about dyslexia.

Thanks for reading,
Abigail Griebelbauer

Inclusive Children's Book Fund

10% of The Passage Press profits from books sold goes to the ICB Fund. This fund provides free inclusive children's books for teachers. For teachers to sign up or for more information, go to our website and click on "ICB Fund".

The Passage Press

Contact information and activity pages are available at **www.thepassagepress.com**

On the page where Darcy is reading aloud in class, the illustration represents her feelings during that time. She created her art masterpiece to show what reading could be for her in the future. Now, it is your turn to be the artist and create what your feelings look like when you are reading. Please go to www.thepassagepress.com for printable copies of this activity sheet.

Here is a coloring page for you. The art frame is
empty so that you can create your own masterpiece.
Please go to www.thepassagepress.com for printable copies of this activity sheet.

Discussion Questions

1. One of Darcy's strengths is her creativity. What is one of your strengths? How do you help others using this strength now? How will you use this strength to help others in the future?

2. Darcy finds reading to be difficult. She is improving with all of her hard work. What is something that you find difficult? How can you help yourself make it less difficult for you? What can you ask others to do that would help make it less difficult?

3. Miss Williams has supported Darcy through her struggles with reading. What are some ways that we can support others, especially when they are struggling with something?

4. Clara was there for Darcy when she thought she didn't win the art fair. Who is someone who made you feel better about a situation that you feel upset or sad? What did they do to make you feel better?

5. Darcy was shocked when she found out that she had won the art fair. When was a time that you were shocked about something fun that happened to you?

Made in the USA
Las Vegas, NV
15 May 2023

72098457R00021